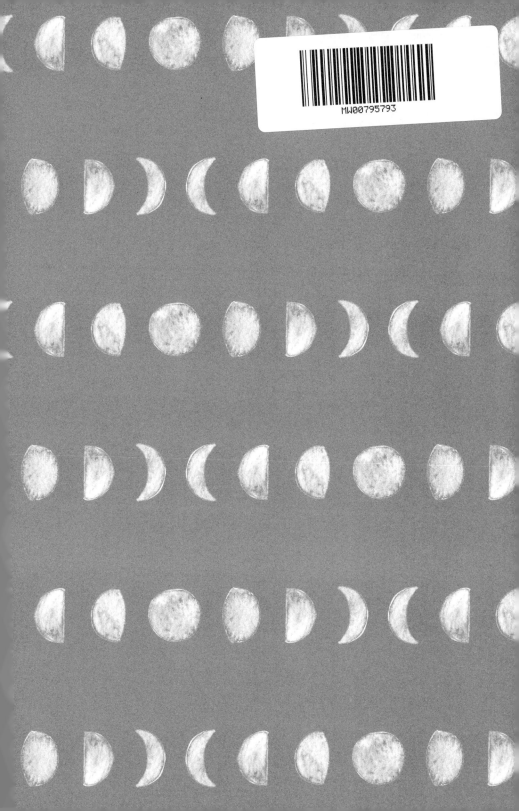

MW00795793

THE
MINDFUL
WITCH

A Daily Journal for Manifesting

a *Truly Magickal Life*

JENN STEVENS

CASTLE POINT BOOKS

NEW YORK

FOR ALL THE BRAVE AND BEAUTIFUL WOMEN IN MY WORLD,
YOU'RE ALL MUCH MORE MAGICAL THAN YOU KNOW. –J.S.

THE MINDFUL WITCH

www.stmartins.com
www.castlepointbooks.com

The Castle Point Books trademark is owned by Castle Point Publishing, LLC.
Castle Point books are published and distributed by St. Martin's Press.

Design by Katie Jennings Campbell and Melissa Gerber

ISBN 978-1-250-23781-1 (paper over board)

Our books may be purchased in bulk for promotional, educational, or business use.
Please contact your local bookseller or the Macmillan Corporate and Premium
Sales Department at 1-800-221-7945, extension 5442, or by email
at MacmillanSpecialMarkets@macmillan.com.

First Edition: September 2019

10 9 8 7 6 5 4 3 2 1

This Magickal
Journal Belongs To:

_____

Contents

INTRODUCTION

THE MODERN WITCH CREATES HER OWN UNIQUE MAGICKAL game as she goes; she's not beholden to any one particular idea about the practice of witchcraft. She embodies the word eclectic, gleaning her inspiration anywhere she finds it, pulling from ancient philosophy books, popular blogs, or her yoga class as she sees fit. Not surprisingly, mindfulness has grown to become a deep source of inspiration for many a modern witch. Living mindfully brings a new level of peace and self-acceptance to anyone trying to stay true to who they are and live their most magickal life.

This journal is designed to help you weave mindfulness into your daily practice of witchcraft and to align you with your true desires so you can manifest them in the world. Begin by describing your relationship with witchcraft and how it has enhanced your life. Allow yourself to be guided through an entire year of magickal, mindful, practice; a year that lets you spend time voicing your thoughts without judgment, declaring your intentions, deepening your craft and your sense of self, and giving thanks to nature and all that inspires you.

Prepare to set a course for the bright future of your own design, leaving what no longer serves you in the past. Fill the pages that follow with the details of your mindful, magickal journey and claim the beautiful and fulfilling life you deserve.

A witch is just a girl
who knows her mind.

—Catherynne M. Valente

My Journey
So Far

FINDING WITCHCRAFT

WITCHCRAFT IS A WAY OF LIFE THAT SUPPORTS THOSE who refuse to live by other people's rules and let life pass them by. Forget the pointy hats and shoes. Forget the broom and the cat and all the stereotypical nonsense. THE MOST IMPORTANT TOOL FOR ANY WITCH IS A STRONG SENSE OF SELF.

As little girls, the world taught us to be the princess rather than the witch. We were the pretty yet helpless girl waiting in the tower for someone to save her. We were supposed to be the good girl, sitting still and quiet as we obeyed all the rules. Instead of waiting for someone else to come along and save us, many of us rejected this idea and grew up looking for ways to take back our power and start saving ourselves.

Being a witch simply means that you've dared to create your own reality! Underneath all the different labels and schools, all witches feel empowered to make their will known to the world.

Describe your own path to discovering witchcraft.

(Be honest! It's not always as noble as we'd like to believe. For example, many of us were initially attracted to the craft by the desire to cast a love spell! While the guy—or girl—may be gone, the pull to witchcraft remained.)

Ever since I was young, I had this intense pull towards the magical side. My mother was a believer & fascinated with its history and encouraged my curiosity. I can remember sketching little drawings of crystal balls, magic wands and creating a crystal guide based on colors. Later, I would hand-make my own runes (which, my mother said: "anything you craft with your own hands will have the most power." In my years, my intuition has grown stronger than ever & my interest in this world of tarot, spells, manifestation, divination and beyond still inspires and excites me.

WITCH, KNOW THYSELF

ONE OF THE MOST INFLUENTIAL pieces of witchcraft advice is *know thyself*, a mantra taken directly from the inscription over the entrance at the oracle of Delphi.

seer

creative

CONJURE UP
5 WORDS OR
SYMBOLS THAT
EXPRESS WHO
YOU TRULY ARE:

dreamer

lover ♥

strong

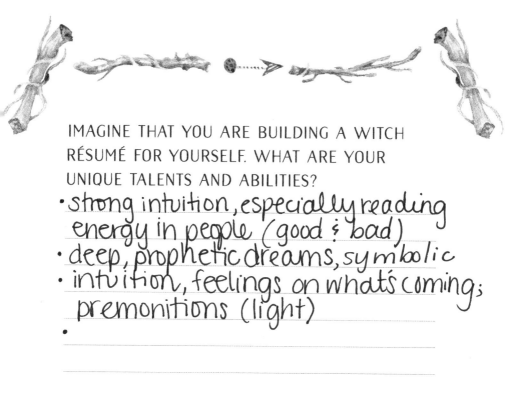

IMAGINE THAT YOU ARE BUILDING A WITCH
RÉSUMÉ FOR YOURSELF. WHAT ARE YOUR
UNIQUE TALENTS AND ABILITIES?

- strong intuition, especially reading energy in people (good & bad)
- deep, prophetic dreams, symbolic
- intuition, feelings on what's coming; premonitions (light)
-

WHAT ARE YOUR WEAKNESSES? (WE ALL
HAVE THEM, BUT BEING AWARE OF THEM
HELPS US KNOW OURSELVES BETTER.)

- beginner with spellwork
- emotional (can cloud work)
- still learning, slow
- slightly afraid: want to keep on a pure path

The Mindful Witch

Mindfulness is the simple practice of noticing our thoughts and feelings in a judgement-free way. It's about noticing our life as it actually happens instead of getting caught up in the past or future. Instead of fighting with reality, it's about accepting how we currently feel and letting those feelings pass. This takes up a lot less energy than denial and resentment!

To Thine Own Self Be True

Always remember that you are the ultimate creator of your practice. If your heart isn't in something, it doesn't matter how pretty you can make it all look on Instagram! There's no authenticity checker for what you see online—but you can be your own authenticity checker. Follow your soul's desires and inspirations and forget about what the rest of the witch world is up to.

!ha! I needed that today

Mindfulness can bring peace to our lives by helping us let go of the past and release our anxiety about the future.

Being mindful of yourself (your emotions, motivations, and desires) is simply a necessary practice for a witch. To have control over anything, you must first have it over yourself. That's where mindfulness can be a crucial addition to your craft.

HOW COULD YOU BENEFIT FROM MINDFULNESS?

Back to a weakness I listed: being emotional. Being more mindful will aid in my emotions, when I'm doing work on something that is "close" to me & can render more emotion.

MINDFULNESS &
THE MODERN WITCH

MINDFULNESS IS PERFECTLY WOVEN INTO EVERYTHING the witch holds dear. While witch traditions vary in their details, a common thread between them is honoring Mother Nature. Watching the moon phases and the cycles of the year are how we connect our magick to ourselves and the world around us. When we honor our natural environment, we are being mindful. Every witch worth her salt knows exactly where the moon is at all times! The more deeply you can connect with Mother Nature, the stronger your practice will be.

Mindfulness goes beyond celebrating the ever-changing natural world. It's also about knowing yourself. Becoming your own best friend is the best thing you can do for your practice—and life in general! And what better way to do that than to learn to sit with your thoughts and get acquainted with yourself and your feelings and desires. All the accoutrements of the craft are lovely to have—but make no mistake: a witch's greatest power is her own mind.

Existing fully in the moment and knowing your body, mind, and soul is the secret to manifesting a truly magickal life.

AWAKEN
THE SENSES

Begin your journey with an introduction to mindfulness. Whether this is a familiar concept to you or a brand-new way of thinking, use the prompts below to practice a heightened sense of awareness.

Notice the room around you.

WHAT ARE YOU HEARING?

the heat blowing in the vents; ice dinking in my glass

FEELING?

calm, reflective, a little tired

SMELLING?

lime from my drink; unwashed hair (ha!) & the smell of this book

Tune in.

WHAT ARE THE STRONGEST EMOTIONS
YOU'RE FEELING RIGHT NOW?

worry about my path (instagram
or something else?) and what my
love path looks like in the future.

HOW DOES YOUR BODY FEEL RIGHT NOW?

tired; poor pillows for sleeping
toe is still broken :'(

WHAT ARE YOU CRAVING OR DESIRING FOR
YOURSELF (PHYSICALLY, EMOTIONALLY, ETC.)?

Physically heal to get healthier
emotionally heal from relationship
issues,
WHAT IS YOUR MIND TRYING TO CONVINCE death.
YOU TO WORRY OR CREATE DRAMA ABOUT?

"Why is my relationship all of a
sudden really good again? Something
must be wrong."

IS THAT WORRY NECESSARY?

No. not until there's something
to tangibly worry about. Need
to let Go & let God.

CREATING
YOUR ALTAR

Every witch needs a sacred space for conducting their rituals and honoring the elements. The altar represents your connection with nature and the divine. It's up to you to create one that fits your life, the occasion, and your mood.

Before beginning your spellwork, take the time to add elements to your altar that reflect how you feel and what you want. Take a mindful moment each day to admire your handiwork and reflect on each object's meaning.

Altars typically include a selection of traditional altar tools: athame, cauldron (or fireproof bowl), wand, and altar bell. It's also common to include representations of the four elements on your altar: earth, air, fire, and water. You can also add personal elements like photos, tchotchkes, and personal heirlooms.

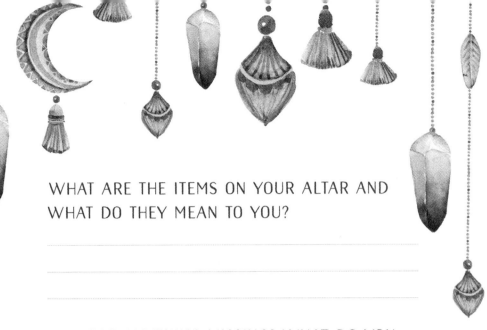

WHAT ARE THE ITEMS ON YOUR ALTAR AND
WHAT DO THEY MEAN TO YOU?

IS THERE ANYTHING MISSING? WHAT DO YOU
FEEL CALLED TO INCORPORATE RIGHT NOW?

PLAN OR DRAW YOUR IDEAL ALTAR BELOW.
WHAT ITEMS BEST REPRESENT YOU?

SPELLS

SPELLCASTING IS PART OF EVERY WITCH'S REPERTOIRE! It's how we make our will manifest.

A traditional spell involves identifying, raising, and directing energy in order to make our intentions take hold in the physical world. It's not a spell unless you have a clear intention.

TO BEGIN, WRITE DOWN THREE THINGS FOR WHICH YOU FEEL GRATEFUL TODAY:

1
2
3

WRITE DOWN THREE INTENTIONS YOU WOULD LIKE TO MANIFEST IN THE NEAR FUTURE USING SPELLS:

1
2
3

RITUALS

RITUAL IS THE BACKBONE OF THE WITCH'S LIFE! Ritual serves multiple purposes in the witch's life: to mark the passing of time and the seasons, to honor a deity or a time of year, and, in combination with spells, to bring about specific changes that you wish to see in the world. Rituals can be short and fast or elaborate and lengthy. They can fall on traditional celebration days or whenever the mood strikes. Rituals are simply the way we communicate gratitude (and sometimes intention) to the unseen world. Embrace them as an outlet for your unique creativity and power.

Creating a ritual is never just a superstitious act. It's always about harnessing your own power into one single focus. The elements of the ritual only have power because *you* made it so!

YOUR RITUALS

WHAT RITUALS DO YOU PRACTICE IN YOUR
EVERYDAY LIFE?

WHAT RITUALS DO YOU PRACTICE TO HONOR NATURE?

WHAT RITUALS HAVE HELPED YOU MANIFEST
CHANGES IN YOUR LIFE?

WHEN AND WHERE DO YOU FEEL MOST POWERFUL?

HOW COULD YOU INCREASE YOUR SENSE OF POWER
THE NEXT TIME YOU CARRY OUT A RITUAL?

THE FOUR ELEMENTS

~~~~~~~~~~~~~~~~~~~~~~~~~~~~~~~

MOST RITUALS HARNESS THE POWER OF NATURE BY
incorporating the four elements.

WHAT DOES EACH ELEMENT REPRESENT TO YOU?

_____
_____
_____
_____
_____

WHAT MAKES YOU GRATEFUL FOR THEM?

_____
_____
_____
_____
_____

FIRE   AIR   WATER   EARTH

If you would be a magician, honor the Earth. Honor life. Love. Know that magic is the birthright of every human being, and wisely use it.

—Scott Cunningham

27

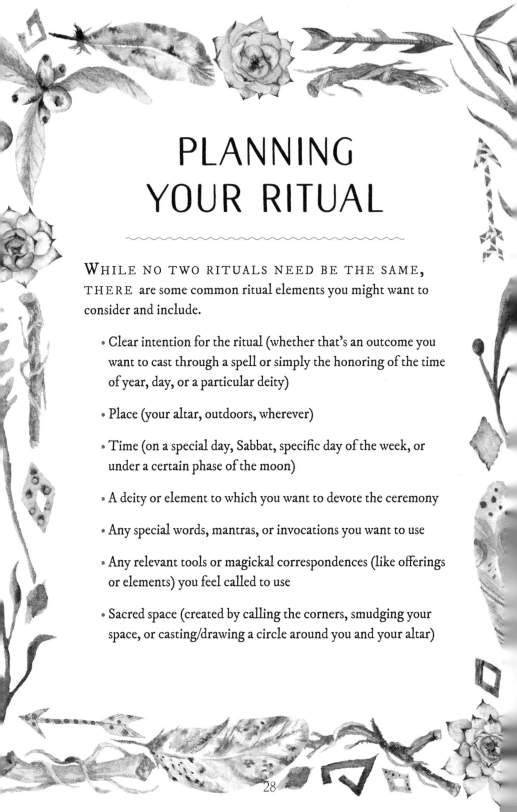

PLANNING
YOUR RITUAL

W HILE NO TWO RITUALS NEED BE THE SAME,
THERE are some common ritual elements you might want to
consider and include.

- Clear intention for the ritual (whether that's an outcome you
  want to cast through a spell or simply the honoring of the time
  of year, day, or a particular deity)

- Place (your altar, outdoors, wherever)

- Time (on a special day, Sabbat, specific day of the week, or
  under a certain phase of the moon)

- A deity or element to which you want to devote the ceremony

- Any special words, mantras, or invocations you want to use

- Any relevant tools or magickal correspondences (like offerings
  or elements) you feel called to use

- Sacred space (created by calling the corners, smudging your
  space, or casting/drawing a circle around you and your altar)

Casting a Circle

Take a few moments to meditate or center yourself before you begin your ritual. Draw a circle around you and your altar (or sacred space). You can build an actual circle with objects (like salt or rocks, for example, if you're outside). Or you can just "draw" the circle around you with a magickal tool (like an athame) or your finger!

MAGICKAL CORRESPONDENCES

WHEN IT COMES TO WITCHCRAFT, YOU HAVE TO LOOK BEYOND the surface. Witches are masters at using correspondences (or symbols) to enhance their magick. They know that everything in the universe has an energetic signature that can help them in their practice. Objects and colors can be useful stand-ins for elements and concepts. Trying to invoke the element of air? Consider placing correspondences like a feather, a fan, or something sky blue on your altar.

As always, your instincts are more powerful than anything! Harness your own intuition and jot some of your own inspired ideas for magickal correspondences here:

The Seasons

Make notes below as you consider symbols and/or colors to use for each season in your rituals.

WINTER ....

FALL ....

SPRING ....

SUMMER ....

(THE MOON CYCLES

THE LUNAR HOLY DAYS (ALSO KNOWN AS ESBATS) celebrate the moon's passage around Earth. Any phase of the moon can be a good time for a ritual or celebration, but each phase has its own power and meaning.

Consider the power and meaning of each moon phase below and write ideas for channeling each phase to manifest your goals.

FULL MOON (LETTING GO OF SOMETHING OR SOMEONE)

WANING (BANISHING SPELLS)

NEW MOON (SETTING NEW INTENTIONS)

WAXING (ATTRACTING SPELLS)

The moon is faithful to its nature
and its power is never diminished.

—Ming-Dao Deng

THE DAYS OF THE WEEK

EVERY DAY OF THE WEEK ALSO REPRESENTS A DEITY.
Gain inspiration from these dieties and spend some time journaling
about each one. What does each day mean to you? What does each deity
represent? Add in any of your own ideas about correspondences as you go.

Sunday: THE SUN GOD, SOL

Monday: GODDESS MOON, MANI'S DAY

Tuesday: MARS, GOD OF WAR, TYR'S DAY

Wednesday: MERCURY, ODIN, THE RAVEN GOD

Thursday: JUPITER, THOR, GOD OF STRENGTH AND STORMS

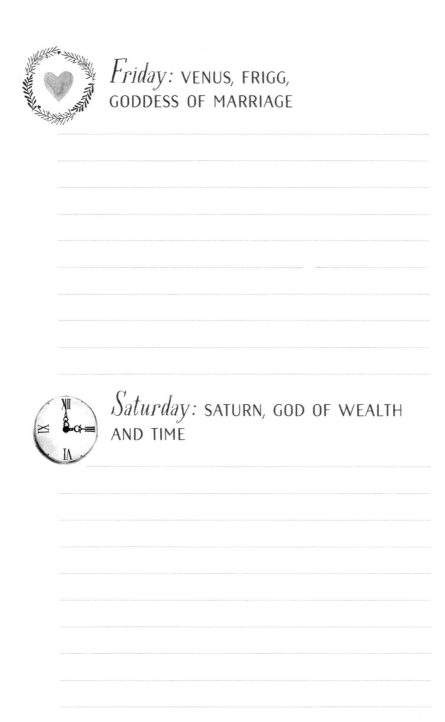

Friday: VENUS, FRIGG, GODDESS OF MARRIAGE

Saturday: SATURN, GOD OF WEALTH AND TIME

PERFORMING RITUALS

1. ASSEMBLE YOUR ELEMENTS, OFFERINGS, AND TOOLS AHEAD OF THE APPOINTED TIME.

For example, collect seasonally appropriate elements from nature or something that relates to the intention you're going to set.

2. CLEANSE THE SPACE.

Smudge, burn incense, or use a bell to cleanse the energy where you're conducting the ritual.

3. CLEANSE YOURSELF.

One way to energetically cleanse yourself is to burn incense and fan the smoke all around your body.

4. CAST A CIRCLE TO CREATE A SACRED SPACE FOR YOUR MAGICK.

Use objects or your finger to draw/mark a circle of protection around you.

Casting a Circle by Hand

There are many ways to cast a circle, but this way is the simplest: Stand in the center of your ritual space. Imagine that you are connecting with the energy of the earth through your feet and also with the energy of the universe through the top of your head. Once you feel this connection, simply point a finger at the ground and spin yourself around 360 degrees while reciting your own version of this: *I now cast this circle for my protection. Please keep all negativity out and let only love come in.*

5. INVOKE YOUR CHOSEN DEITY OR ELEMENT.

For example, if you're casting a love spell you might want to dedicate your ritual to the Goddess Venus.

6. CONDUCT THE RITUAL OR SPELL.

Go minimal and simply state your intention or add more elements, as you see fit.

7. THANK THE DEITY.

If you've invoked the Goddess Venus, give her a big thank-you for helping with your magickal petition. Something simple like "Thank you! Blessed be and so it is" will do the trick.

8. TAKE DOWN THE CIRCLE.

The final step is to physically open and release the circle.

Taking Down the Circle by Hand

At the close of a ritual, connect your energy once again with the earth and sky. Then point your finger at the ground and turn in a clockwise direction while saying something like *The circle is open but never broken. Merry meet, merry part, and merry meet again.* Imagine that the energy protecting you is being released back into the ether and trust that your magick is now complete.

THE WITCH'S CALENDAR

No MATTER WHAT KIND OF WITCH YOU ARE (and there are many kinds!) there's one common thread among us: true respect and gratitude for Mother Nature herself.

The seasons around us are forever changing, and the witch marks the passing of time through celebrating these cycles. There is no good or bad in nature. Each season shines in its own particular way.

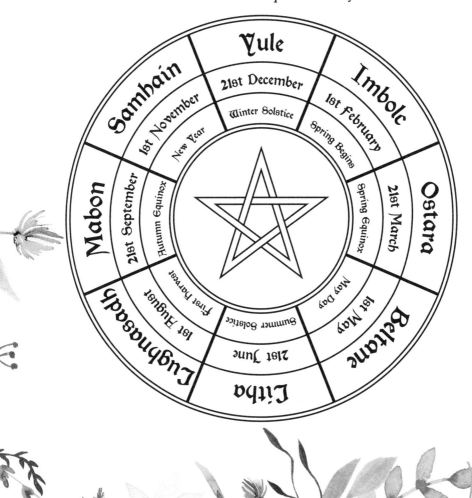

The Witch's Calendar (also called the Wiccan Calendar or the Wheel of the Year) marks the passing of time through the natural cycles of nature. It shows eight seasonal holidays, or Sabbats. Observing these Sabbats is described as *spinning the wheel.*

The Sabbats

The Sabbats are the traditional Wiccan holy days of the year and they symbolize the cycle of nature: birth, growth, death, rebirth. Four of the Sabbats fall on the equinoxes and solstices (Yule, Ostara, Litha, and Mabon), while the remaining four fall at the midway points (Imbolc, Beltane, Lammas, and Samhain).

Celebrating these days through rituals and offerings is referred to as turning the wheel. Each holiday gives us the opportunity to celebrate both nature and the passing of time.

WHAT DO YOU WANT MOST OUT
OF LIFE THIS COMING YEAR?

WHO ARE YOU HOPING
TO BE ONE YEAR FROM NOW?

HOW CAN YOU BE MORE AUTHENTICALLY
YOU DURING THIS PROCESS?

MINDFUL MEDITATION

SOMETIMES, THE BEST WAY TO FIND THE ANSWERS YOU'RE seeking and feel free and authentic is to take pause and meditate. Here is one technique to help you connect to the present and work meditation into your day. All it takes is a few moments of quietly noticing what's going on in and around you.

STEP 1:
Find a quiet, comfortable place to sit down.

STEP 2:
Set a timer. You don't have to meditate for an hour for it to be effective! Start with 5 or 10 minutes.

STEP 3:
Make sure you're sitting with a straight back and that you feel comfortable.

STEP 4:
Take three deep breaths then let your breathing return to normal. Notice the natural rhythm of your breath going in and out.

STEP 5:
You don't have to completely clear your mind of thoughts, but simply acknowledge them and let them pass. When you notice them taking over, come back to noticing your body and breathing.

A little magic can take you a long way.

—Roald Dahl

My Mindful, Magickal Year Ahead

JANUARY
THE WOLF MOON

THIS FULL MOON IS NAMED for the hungry wolves howling outside villages. This is the time where most of us are nestled safely indoors under a pile of comforters, preferably with snacks and Netflix.

Naturally, this is a low-energy time— making it an ideal time for mindfulness, introspection, and planning for the year ahead!

WHAT DOES THE MONTH OF JANUARY MEAN TO YOU?

WHAT ARE YOU GRATEFUL FOR AT THIS TIME?

46

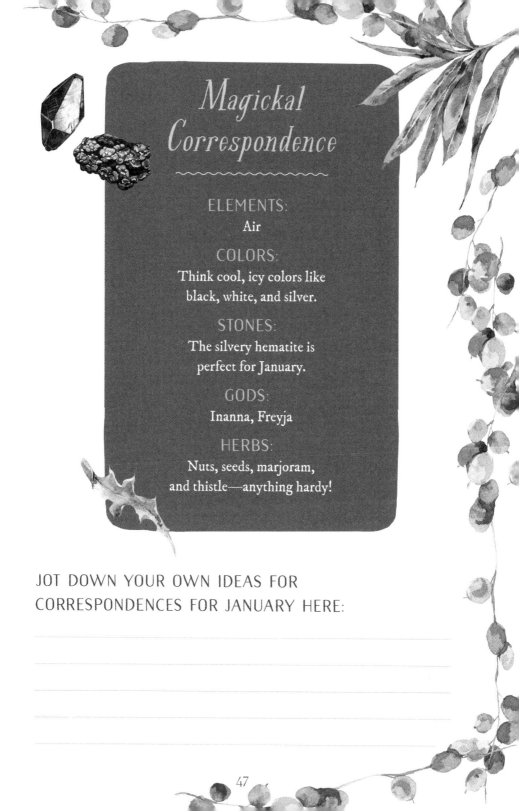

Magickal Correspondence

ELEMENTS:
Air

COLORS:
Think cool, icy colors like
black, white, and silver.

STONES:
The silvery hematite is
perfect for January.

GODS:
Inanna, Freyja

HERBS:
Nuts, seeds, marjoram,
and thistle—anything hardy!

JOT DOWN YOUR OWN IDEAS FOR
CORRESPONDENCES FOR JANUARY HERE:

NEW MOON
IN CAPRICORN

CAPRICORN, THE SIGN OF THE GOAT, IS ALL ABOUT
being productive and focused. What better sign for the beginning of the
year? January signals that it's time to put your head down and make some
serious progress on whatever it is you happen to be working toward. Keep
moving upward one step at a time, and you'll have scaled your dreams in no
time at all! Use this time to reflect on new ideas and start making your plan
of attack.

WHICH PERSONAL DREAMS OR GOALS ARE YOU
FOCUSING MOST OF YOUR EFFORTS ON ACHIEVING?

WHAT CONSISTENT ACTIONS CAN YOU
START TO TAKE TOWARD YOUR GOALS?

NEW MOON IN CAPRICORN
INTENTIONS

TAKE A FEW MINDFUL MOMENTS TO REFLECT ON WHERE you are now before you decide where to go next. Then set a few intentions for this new moon.

WISH 1:

_____

_____

_____

WISH 2:

_____

_____

_____

WISH 3:

_____

_____

_____

If we pursue a spiritual path in depth, then it changes who and what we are. There is no turning back. We can only move forward.

—Vivianne Crowley

JANUARY MINDFULNESS & REFLECTIONS

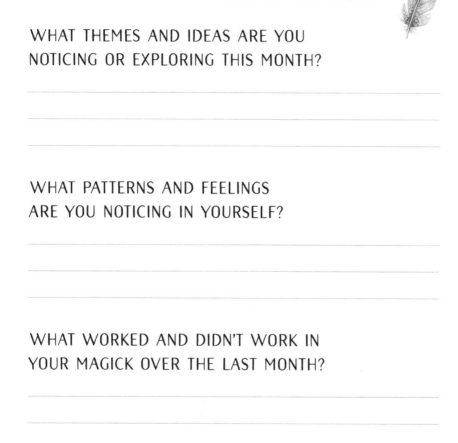

WHAT THEMES AND IDEAS ARE YOU
NOTICING OR EXPLORING THIS MONTH?

WHAT PATTERNS AND FEELINGS
ARE YOU NOTICING IN YOURSELF?

WHAT WORKED AND DIDN'T WORK IN
YOUR MAGICK OVER THE LAST MONTH?

FEBRUARY
THE HUNGER MOON

THIS FULL MOON COMES WHEN THE SNOW IS AT ITS heaviest. The cold days of February can be a difficult time, so this month reminds us to be grateful for our modern fortunes.

It's also a beautiful reminder to trust in the future. New life is coming forth, even though we may not be able to see it yet!

It's time to get out into nature, despite the cold.

 *Take part in the season and plant some seeds (outdoors if the climate allows; indoors if it doesn't).*

WHAT DOES THE MONTH OF FEBRUARY MEAN TO YOU?

WHAT ARE YOU GRATEFUL FOR AT THIS TIME?

JOT DOWN YOUR OWN IDEAS FOR
CORRESPONDENCES FOR FEBRUARY HERE:

Magickal Correspondence

ELEMENTS:
Fire

COLORS:
Rich, cool tones like purple and blue are perfect for February.

STONES:
Rose quartz, jasper, and amethyst are beautiful representations of
the season.

GODS:
Brigid, Juno, and Mars are all associated with this time of year.

HERBS:
Sage, hyssop, and myrrh

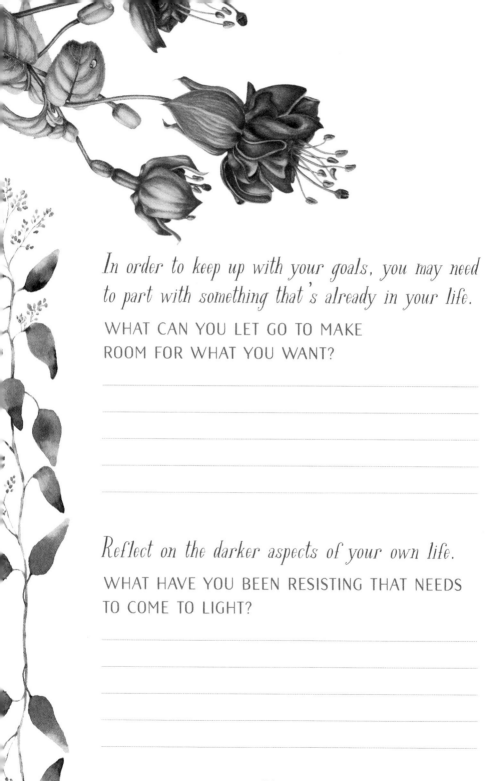

In order to keep up with your goals, you may need to part with something that's already in your life.

WHAT CAN YOU LET GO TO MAKE
ROOM FOR WHAT YOU WANT?

_____

_____

_____

_____

_____

Reflect on the darker aspects of your own life.

WHAT HAVE YOU BEEN RESISTING THAT NEEDS
TO COME TO LIGHT?

_____

_____

_____

_____

What we think, we become.
What we feel, we attract.
What we imagine, we create.

NEW MOON
IN AQUARIUS

AIRY AQUARIUS INVITES US TO THINK OUTSIDE
the box. This rule-breaking sign reminds us to dance to our own
beat. Keep a lookout for new connections that inspire your inner
creativity. Aquarians are natural visionaries who enjoy bringing
people together, so embrace that attitude this month.

Drop in a listen.

WHAT ARE YOUR FEELINGS TELLING YOU
RIGHT NOW? REMEMBER, THEY ARE ALWAYS
MORE IMPORTANT THAN YOUR THOUGHTS.

Sabbat: Imbolc

As the days turn slowly brighter, it's time to prepare for springtime ahead. Imbolc is a time to celebrate Brigid, the Goddess of Healing and Fire. This is the Sabbat of hidden potential, renewal, and a time for emotional and physical spring cleaning! It's time to shake out the energy of the winter to prepare for the coming season of growth.

Brigid Activities:

1. SPRING CLEAN YOUR HOME FROM TOP TO BOTTOM.

2. PROTECT YOUR ENERGY AND CONSERVE IT FOR WHAT'S MOST IMPORTANT TO YOU! START SAYING NO TO ENGAGEMENTS THAT DON'T LIGHT YOU UP OR THAT MAKE YOU RESENTFUL.

NEW MOON IN AQUARIUS
INTENTIONS

TAKE A FEW MINDFUL MOMENTS TO REFLECT ON WHERE
you are now before you decide where to go next. Then set a few intentions
for this new moon.

WISH 1:

_____

_____

WISH 2:

_____

_____

WISH 3:

_____

_____

FEBRUARY MINDFULNESS
& REFLECTIONS

WHAT THEMES & IDEAS ARE YOU
NOTICING OR EXPLORING THIS MONTH?

WHAT PATTERNS AND FEELINGS
ARE YOU NOTICING IN YOURSELF?

WHAT WORKED & DIDN'T WORK IN
YOUR MAGICK OVER THE LAST MONTH?

MARCH
THE SAP MOON

THIS MOON ARRIVES AS THE GROUND BEGINS TO SOFTEN and the maple sap begins to flow from the trees! While spring isn't in full bloom just yet, this is a time to be thankful for the return of life to the earth. It's a time to evolve and notice changes happening all around you. It's also a time to see past illusions to the realities they are hiding.

WHAT DOES THE MONTH OF MARCH MEAN TO YOU?

FOR WHAT ARE YOU GRATEFUL AT THIS TIME?

Magickal Correspondence

ELEMENT:
Water

COLORS:
Easter colors like green, yellow, or lilac.

STONES:
Aquamarine or bloodstone

GODS:
This is a time to celebrate strong women like Isis,
Artemis, and Cybele.

HERBS:
Spring herbs like pennyroyal,
apple blossom

JOT DOWN YOUR OWN IDEAS FOR
CORRESPONDENCES FOR MARCH HERE:

*Do whatever
brings you
to life.*

—Elizabeth Gilbert

Sabbat: Ostara

(MARCH 20 OR 21)

Light has won its victory against the dark! The nights will now begin to shrink as the days grow longer. Go for a mindful walk in the park and notice how it feels to connect to Mother Nature.

On this vernal equinox, both day and night lie in perfect equilibrium. It's a beautiful time to celebrate fertility, new beginnings, and renewal. While nature is not in bloom yet, the growing season is about to begin.

How do you celebrate or honor the spring equinox?

NEW MOON IN PISCES

MYSTERIOUS PISCES IS HERE THIS MONTH TO REMIND us to dream. This watery energy is a time of heightened emotions. But don't be tempted to resist them! Lean into them and figure out what they're here to show you.

WHAT'S TRIGGERING YOUR EMOTIONS RIGHT NOW?

WHAT ARE YOUR EMOTIONS TELLING YOU?

HOW CAN YOU CULTIVATE MORE
COMPASSION FOR YOURSELF?

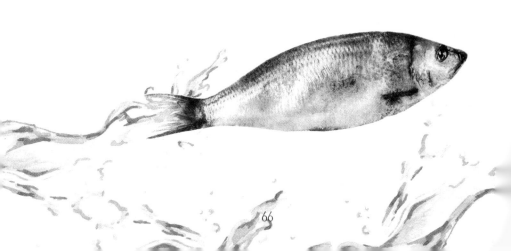

NEW MOON IN PISCES
INTENTIONS

TAKE A FEW MINDFUL MOMENTS TO REFLECT ON WHERE
you are now before you decide where to go next. Then set a few intentions
for this new moon.

WISH 1:

WISH 2:

WISH 3:

MARCH MINDFULNESS
& REFLECTIONS

WHAT THEMES & IDEAS ARE YOU
NOTICING OR EXPLORING THIS MONTH?

_____

_____

_____

WHAT PATTERNS AND FEELINGS
ARE YOU NOTICING IN YOURSELF?

_____

_____

_____

WHAT WORKED & DIDN'T WORK IN
YOUR MAGICK OVER THE LAST MONTH?

_____

_____

_____

Being a witch isn't what you do;
it's who you are.

APRIL
THE WIND MOON

APRIL IS A NATURALLY STORMY TIME! THE SPRING tension between the passing cold and the coming heat creates the traditional rains—but also winds. These are the winds of change. April is a time to plant the seeds of new beginnings.

WHAT DOES THE MONTH OF APRIL MEAN TO YOU?

_____

_____

_____

WHAT ARE YOU GRATEFUL FOR AT THIS TIME?

_____

_____

WHAT IDEAS ARE YOU FORMING?

_____
_____
_____
_____
_____

WHAT CHANGES WOULD
YOU LIKE TO SET IN MOTION?

_____
_____
_____
_____
_____
_____

Magickal Correspondence

ELEMENT:
Air

COLORS:
Bright primary colors like red or yellow
are associated with spring.

STONES:
Quartz, selenite, angelite

GODS/GODDESSES:
Ishtar, Venus, and Herne
represent the blossoming of the earth.

HERBS:
Milkweed, fennel, dandelion, and dill
represent seeds ready to dive back into the earth.

JOT DOWN YOUR OWN IDEAS FOR CORRESPONDENCES
FOR APRIL HERE:

Those who don't believe in magic will never find it.

—Roald Dahl

NEW MOON IN ARIES

THIS MONTH ARIES, THE RAM, ARRIVES WITH ITS independent headstrong spirit. This the perfect time to move your body (dance, go running), or even move into a new home. An Aries doesn't sit around wondering—she takes action now! So this is your moment to indulge in spontaneity and pure expression. Make note of what your body or soul is craving to do right now. Take any bumps in the road in stride!

April Activity

Let loose and get in touch with your body and soul. Throw on your favorite music and have a ten-minute dance party in your bedroom.

NEW MOON IN ARIES
INTENTIONS

TAKE A FEW MINDFUL MOMENTS TO REFLECT ON WHERE
you are now before you decide where to go next. Then set a few intentions
for this new moon.

WISH 1:

WISH 2:

WISH 3:

APRIL MINDFULNESS
& REFLECTIONS

WHAT THEMES & IDEAS ARE YOU
NOTICING OR EXPLORING THIS MONTH?

WHAT PATTERNS AND FEELINGS
ARE YOU NOTICING IN YOURSELF?

WHAT WORKED & DIDN'T WORK IN
YOUR MAGICK OVER THE LAST MONTH?

MAY
THE FLOWER MOON

WHAT A BEAUTIFUL TIME OF YEAR! SPRING IS OFFICIALLY here and the flowers are finally in bloom. It's a time of fresh new beginnings. It's time to plant seeds for the summer months ahead. This is a time of fertility and growth for all.

WHAT DOES THE MONTH OF MAY MEAN TO YOU?

WHAT ARE YOU GRATEFUL FOR AT THIS TIME?

_____

_____

_____

_____

HOW CAN YOU CREATE MORE
ABUNDANCE IN YOUR LIFE?

_____

_____

_____

_____

WHAT DO YOU NEED TO TEND IN YOUR OWN
PERSONAL GARDEN THAT YOU CAN REAP THE
RESULTS FROM LATER?

_____

_____

_____

_____

...in Nature, I felt everything
I should feel in church but never
did. Walking in the woods, I felt in
touch with the universe and with the
spirit of the universe.

—Alice Walker

Magickal
Correspondence

ELEMENT:
Fire

COLORS:
Go warm with colors like red, yellow,
and orange to represent the sun as it draws nearer to Earth.

STONES:
Warm-colored stones like garnet, amber, and ruby
are associated with the fertility of the occasion.

GODS:
Flora and Cerrunos are associated with
the blossoming forest and burgeoning crops.

HERBS:
Fiery spices like cinnamon as well as
mint are perfect for Beltane.

JOT DOWN YOUR OWN IDEAS FOR
CORRESPONDENCES FOR MAY HERE:

Sabbat: Beltane

(MAY 1)

Beltane marks the marriage between the God and Goddess. This ancient fertility festival marks the beginning of the planting cycle. Dedicating this celebration to the gods was a way of ensuring a bountiful harvest.

Get inspired by the light-hearted joy of Beltane!

- Throw yourself a dance party (private or public—your choice!).

- Make flower crowns.

- Create an actual maypole.

NEW MOON IN TAURUS

EARTHY TAURUS INVITES US TO CELEBRATE EARTHLY pleasures. It's a time to celebrate both beauty and pleasure so feel free to book a table at that decadent new Italian place or buy yourself a favorite special bottle of wine. Just be aware not to overdo things!

HOW CAN YOU INDULGE IN THIS PLEASURABLE TAUREAN ENERGY?

_____

_____

_____

WHAT CAN YOU START DOING DAILY TO REMIND YOURSELF OF THE POWER OF PLEASURE?

_____

_____

_____

_____

NEW MOON IN TAURUS
INTENTIONS

TAKE A FEW MINDFUL MOMENTS TO REFLECT ON WHERE you are now before you decide where to go next. Then set a few intentions for this new moon.

WISH 1:

WISH 2:

WISH 3:

MAY MINDFULNESS
& REFLECTIONS

WHAT THEMES & IDEAS ARE YOU
NOTICING OR EXPLORING THIS MONTH?

WHAT PATTERNS AND FEELINGS
ARE YOU NOTICING IN YOURSELF?

WHAT WORKED & DIDN'T WORK IN
YOUR MAGICK OVER THE LAST MONTH?

WHAT DO YOU WANT TO WORK
ON OR INCORPORATE NEXT?

JUNE
ROSE MOON

IT'S TIME TO STOP AND SMELL THE ROSES! THE MOST beautiful flower is in full blossom right now. This moon is a wonderful time to integrate your recent challenges with your existing wisdom. Take some time to reflect on your life's journey and where it appears to be heading next. This is a time for truth and taking self-awareness and strength to the next level.

WHAT DOES THE MONTH OF JUNE MEAN TO YOU?

WHAT ARE YOU GRATEFUL FOR AT THIS TIME?

Magickal Correspondence

ELEMENT:
Earth

COLORS:
Harness the colors of the sun with gold, orange, and yellow.

STONES:
Choose warm stones like topaz and agate.

GODS:
Isis, Persephone, and Cerridwen

HERBS:
Skullcap, mugwort, and parsley are excellent choices.

JOT DOWN YOUR OWN IDEAS FOR
CORRESPONDENCES FOR JUNE HERE:

There's a little
witch in all of us.

—Alice Hoffman, *Practical Magic*

Sabbat: Litha

(June 21)

Time to celebrate the light! Midsummer, or Litha, is the shortest night of the year, but also signals a return to the darkness as autumn approaches. The crops have been planted and nature has reached her natural fullness. This joyous time reminds us to live in the moment and appreciate nature's abundance.

Let midsummer inspire you:

• Weed and tend to your garden.

• Eat some honey (or use it in your ritual).

• Take some time to bask in the sun!
(Or put your tools out in the sun for an energetic bath.)

Real magic is not about gaining power over others: it is about gaining power over yourself.

—Rosemary Guiley

NEW MOON IN GEMINI

GEMINI IS A TIME OF HEIGHTENED COMMUNICATION.
Write that letter you've had on your to-do list or reach out to clear the air
with a friend. Take advantage of this time when words come so easy.

As this is the sign of the Twins, you might also find yourself drawn in two
opposing directions. While this can be confusing at first, learn to embrace
your dual nature! We all have the potential to be many things at the exact
same time.

NEW MOON IN GEMINI
INTENTIONS

TAKE A FEW MINDFUL MOMENTS TO REFLECT ON WHERE you are now before you decide where to go next. Then set a few intentions for this new moon.

WISH 1:

WISH 2:

WISH 3:

JUNE MINDFULNESS & REFLECTIONS

WHAT THEMES & IDEAS ARE YOU
NOTICING OR EXPLORING THIS MONTH?

_____

_____

_____

_____

WHAT PATTERNS AND FEELINGS
ARE YOU NOTICING IN YOURSELF?

_____

_____

_____

_____

WHAT WORKED & DIDN'T WORK IN
YOUR MAGICK OVER THE LAST MONTH?

_____

_____

_____

_____

JULY
THUNDER MOON

THE HOTTEST DAYS OF THE YEAR CREATE A HUGE AMOUNT of energy. That energy naturally unleashes itself through frequent thunderstorms this month. This is a beautiful reminder to let ourselves cool off before we explode! So don't let the summer rush overwhelm you. This is a time where we often need more self-care than ever.

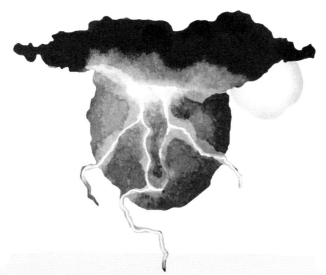

Thunder Moon Activities

- Harvest flower or herbs from your garden.
- Pay close attention to your dreams this month. (They'll be extra potent right now!)
- Try out divination methods, like scrying.

WHAT DOES THE MONTH OF JULY MEAN TO YOU?

WHAT ARE YOU GRATEFUL FOR AT THIS TIME?

Magickal Correspondence

ELEMENT:
Water

COLORS:
Go for airy blue-gray, green, and silver.

STONES:
White agate, opals, pearls, and moonstone
are all wonderful choices.

GODS:
Venus, Athena, Juno, and Nephthys

HERBS:
Mugwort, lemon balm, and hyssop
are wonderful seasonal choices.

JOT DOWN YOUR OWN IDEAS FOR
CORRESPONDENCES FOR JULY HERE:

As above, so below.

NEW MOON IN CANCER

THE NEW MOON IN CANCER INVITES US TO TURN OUR attention inward. Intuitive, caring, and sometimes moody, this sign signals a time of heightened emotions. But whatever you do, don't fight the feelings! Sink into them and allow them to teach you about what needs to be healed.

Embrace your heightened emotions this month!

• Call up your mom (or any other caregiver) and reconnect.

• Write yourself a big, juicy letter of appreciation. (If that seems weird, all the better!)

• Stay home and watch your favorite tearjerker. (All the feels!)

NEW MOON IN CANCER
INTENTIONS

TAKE A FEW MINDFUL MOMENTS TO REFLECT ON WHERE you are now before you decide where to go next. Then set a few intentions for this new moon.

WISH 1:

WISH 2:

WISH 3:

JULY MINDFULNESS & REFLECTIONS

WHAT THEMES & IDEAS ARE YOU
NOTICING OR EXPLORING THIS MONTH?

WHAT PATTERNS AND FEELINGS
ARE YOU NOTICING IN YOURSELF?

WHAT WORKED & DIDN'T WORK IN
YOUR MAGICK OVER THE LAST MONTH?

AUGUST
THE GRAIN MOON

THE GRAIN MOON REMINDS US TO START HARVESTING the fruit of our labor to last over the winter. The fields are full and all of our hard work has come to fruition! This is a beautiful reminder to reap the rewards of what you've created for yourself so far this year.

WHAT DOES THE MONTH OF AUGUST MEAN TO YOU?

_____

_____

_____

_____

WHAT ARE YOU GRATEFUL FOR AT THIS TIME?

_____

_____

_____

_____

TAKE SOME TIME TO REFLECT. WHAT RESULTS ARE
YOU SEEING FROM NEW PROJECTS OR INTERESTS?

_____

_____

_____

_____

WHAT SACRIFICES CAN YOU MAKE NOW THAT WILL
BRING YOU REWARD LATER ON?

_____

_____

_____

_____

Magic doesn't suit everyone.
Only those prepared to take full
responsibility for themselves
should apply.

—Peter J. Carroll

Magickal Correspondence

ELEMENT:
Fire

COLORS:
Warm colors like red, yellow, and orange evoke Leo's energy.

STONES:
Think warm colors like carnelian, tiger's eye, and garnet.

GODS:
August is the right time to invoke the most
powerful gods like Mars, Thoth, Hecate, and Hathor.

HERBS:
Rosemary, chamomile, and basil

JOT DOWN YOUR OWN IDEAS FOR
CORRESPONDENCES FOR AUGUST HERE:

Sabbat: Lammas

(AUGUST 1ST)

Lammas, also referred to as Lughnasad, is a celebration for the gods of the harvest. While it was a time for abundance, it was also a time of fear that the crops wouldn't be enough. This Sabbat is all about facing our fears and taking any action we need to protect ourselves.

Get in the Spirit of Lammas:

• Add some of the bounty of the harvest (like berries) to your altar.

• Make some festive candleholders out of apples.

NEW MOON IN LEO

LEO IS THE ZODIAC'S SUPERSTAR! IT'S A TIME TO TUNE into your heart-centered energy (the heart of the Lion). Roar your way through the month by allowing your gifts to shine bright. It's a time to revel in both your passion and the spotlight. So even if you're not used to it, it's time to put yourself out there.

NEW MOON IN LEO
INTENTIONS

~~~~~~~~~~~~~~~~~~~~~~~~~~~~~~~~~~~~

TAKE A FEW MINDFUL MOMENTS TO REFLECT ON WHERE
you are now before you decide where to go next. Then set a few intentions
for this new moon.

WISH 1:

_____

_____

_____

WISH 2:

_____

_____

_____

WISH 3:

_____

_____

_____

AUGUST MINDFULNESS
& REFLECTIONS

WHAT THEMES & IDEAS ARE YOU
NOTICING OR EXPLORING THIS MONTH?

WHAT PATTERNS AND FEELINGS
ARE YOU NOTICING IN YOURSELF?

WHAT WORKED & DIDN'T WORK IN
YOUR MAGICK OVER THE LAST MONTH?

SEPTEMBER
THE HARVEST MOON

LOOK UP! THE BEAUTIFUL HARVEST MOON IS THE brightest moon of the year. It's thought to be bright enough to allow for harvesting even at night. It's the perfect time to celebrate the bounty of the harvest and the generosity of Mother Earth herself for providing this miracle.

Take the time to be grateful for all you've accomplished this year and be sure to acknowledge your own hard work! It's time to revel in what you've created.

WHAT DOES THE MONTH OF SEPTEMBER MEAN TO YOU?

WHAT ARE YOU MOST GRATEFUL
FOR IN THIS PAST YEAR?

LOOK BACK OVER ALL THAT YOU'VE DONE THIS
YEAR. HOW CAN YOU REWARD YOURSELF FOR
COMING THIS FAR?

WHAT NEW IDEAS ARE COMING FORTH
AT THIS TIME?

Magickal Correspondence

ELEMENT:
Earth

COLORS:
Earthy tones of browns and greens

STONES:
Warm colors like citrine, peridot, and bloodstone
beautifully symbolize the falling leaves.

GODS:
Freyja and Demeter are ideal
choices to honor the harvest.

HERBS:
Wheat, witch hazel, valerian, and skullcap
are perfect seasonal choices for September.

JOT DOWN YOUR OWN IDEAS FOR
CORRESPONDENCES FOR SEPTEMBER HERE:

That's the thing about magic.
You've got to know it's still
here, all around us, or it just
stays invisible for you.

—Charles de Lint

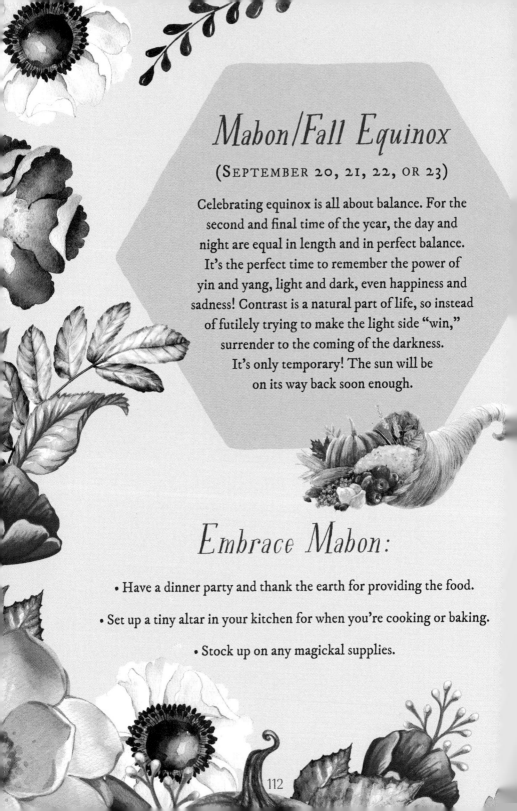

Mabon/Fall Equinox

(SEPTEMBER 20, 21, 22, OR 23)

Celebrating equinox is all about balance. For the second and final time of the year, the day and night are equal in length and in perfect balance. It's the perfect time to remember the power of yin and yang, light and dark, even happiness and sadness! Contrast is a natural part of life, so instead of futilely trying to make the light side "win," surrender to the coming of the darkness. It's only temporary! The sun will be on its way back soon enough.

Embrace Mabon:

- Have a dinner party and thank the earth for providing the food.

- Set up a tiny altar in your kitchen for when you're cooking or baking.

- Stock up on any magickal supplies.

NEW MOON IN VIRGO

NATURALLY, VIRGO ENERGY IS A PERFECT FIT FOR THE beginning of the school year! This time is all about organization, in both your physical and mental space. It's the perfect time to shake out the cobwebs and perhaps to start facing what you've been neglecting or unwilling to face.

NEW MOON IN VIRGO
INTENTIONS

Take a few mindful moments to reflect on WHERE you are now before you decide where to go next. Then set a few intentions for this new moon.

WISH 1:

WISH 2:

WISH 3:

SEPTEMBER MINDFULNESS & REFLECTIONS

WHAT THEMES & IDEAS ARE YOU NOTICING OR EXPLORING THIS MONTH?

WHAT PATTERNS AND FEELINGS ARE YOU NOTICING IN YOURSELF?

WHAT WORKED & DIDN'T WORK IN YOUR MAGICK OVER THE LAST MONTH?

OCTOBER
THE HUNTER'S MOON

TRADITIONALLY, THIS IS THE TIME TO HUNT FOR ANIMALS before they disappear to hibernate for the cold season. Now is the time to seek out and build up provisions for the long winter ahead.

But don't worry, vegan friends! You don't need to actually hunt this month. Think of this as the perfect moment to prepare for the coming cold and ready yourself for the holidays that are around the corner. It's time to ensure that your house is in order so that you can face whatever's coming next.

WHAT DOES THE MONTH OF OCTOBER MEAN TO YOU?

WHAT ARE YOU GRATEFUL FOR AT THIS TIME?

We might not be reaping the harvest ourselves! But October is a great time to check in with the most recent fruits of your labor.

WHAT HAVE YOU SUCCESSFULLY MANIFESTED RECENTLY?

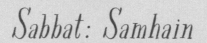

Sabbat: Samhain

(OCTOBER 31 OR NOVEMBER 1)

Here's one holiday where witches can get deep and dark!
Samhain is one of the most important days of the year for
the witch. On this Sabbat, the veil between the human
world and spirit world is at its thinnest. It's the perfect
time to celebrate a bountiful harvest as well as to honor
the ancestors who have already moved on.

Celebrate Samhain by connecting with the spirit world:

- Have a bonfire
(or light candles).

- Write a letter to a deceased love one
(or leave them offerings).

- Hold a seance or work
on your divination.

The first time I
called myself a "Witch"
was the most magickal
moment of my life.

—Margot Adler

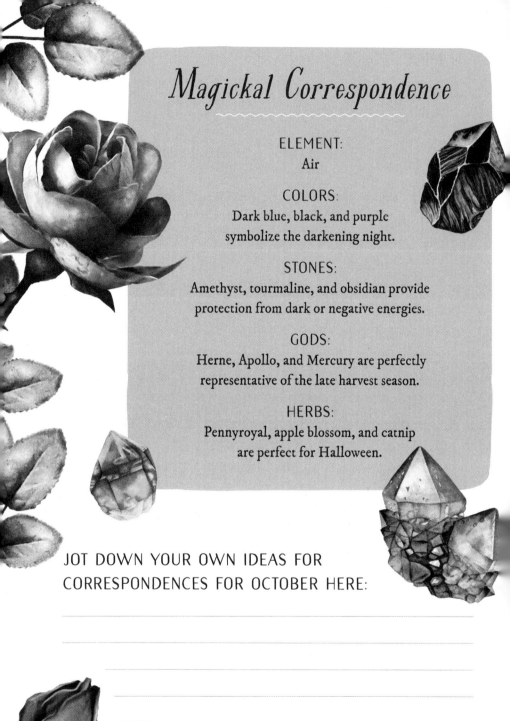

Magickal Correspondence

ELEMENT:
Air

COLORS:
Dark blue, black, and purple
symbolize the darkening night.

STONES:
Amethyst, tourmaline, and obsidian provide
protection from dark or negative energies.

GODS:
Herne, Apollo, and Mercury are perfectly
representative of the late harvest season.

HERBS:
Pennyroyal, apple blossom, and catnip
are perfect for Halloween.

JOT DOWN YOUR OWN IDEAS FOR
CORRESPONDENCES FOR OCTOBER HERE:

_____

_____

_____

_____

NEW MOON IN LIBRA

LIBRA IS ALL ABOUT BALANCE! WE ALL CONTAIN
dualities: light and dark, masculine and feminine. Integrating those
dualities is a way to come into your authentic power. Libra is also
ruled by the planet Venus, making this time extra potent for your
romantic life. But don't forget to indulge in self-love as well!

Consider your life and all its various elements (work, play,
friendships, etc.). Where have you fallen out of balance?

WHAT CAN YOU DO TO CREATE BOUNDARIES THAT
WILL KEEP YOU WELL BALANCED?

NEW MOON IN LIBRA
INTENTIONS

~~~~~~~~~~~~~~~~~~~~~~~~~~~~~~

TAKE A FEW MINDFUL MOMENTS TO REFLECT ON where you are now before you decide where to go next. Then set a few intentions for this new moon.

WISH 1:

WISH 2:

WISH 3:

OCTOBER MINDFULNESS
& REFLECTIONS

WHAT THEMES & IDEAS ARE YOU
NOTICING OR EXPLORING THIS MONTH?

WHAT PATTERNS AND FEELINGS ARE YOU NOTICING
IN YOURSELF?

WHAT WORKED & DIDN'T WORK IN YOUR MAGICK
OVER THE LAST MONTH?

I have been and still
am a seeker, but I
have ceased to question
stars and books; I
have begun to listen to
the teaching my blood
whispers to me.

—Hermann Hesse

NOVEMBER
THE BEAVER MOON

TRADITIONALLY SPEAKING, AT THE END OF THIS moon the beavers would be sleeping and the waters would have frozen over for the winter. This moon signals one final opportunity to strengthen yourself for the winter ahead.

This is a time to wrap up any lingering projects from the spring or summer. It's also a natural time to slow down and indulge your body's need for extra sleep and reset.

Beaver Moon Activities

- Stock your pantry with all your favorite essentials.
- Revel in solitude and take more time to journal.
- Thank the moon for lighting up the darkness of the night.

WHAT DOES THE MONTH OF NOVEMBER MEAN TO YOU?

WHAT ARE YOU GRATEFUL FOR AT THIS TIME?

Magickal Correspondence

ELEMENT:
Water

COLORS:
Blue, gray, and sea-green

STONES:
Lapis lazuli, topaz, and turquoise

GODS:
Hecate, Kali, Lakshmi, and Osiris

HERBS:
Fennel, borage, and verbena

JOT DOWN YOUR OWN IDEAS FOR
CORRESPONDENCES FOR NOVEMBER HERE:

NEW MOON
IN SCORPIO

THE SCORPIO SEASON IS ALL ABOUT THE MOST extreme parts of life: sex, death, and transformation. But this time isn't as scary as it sounds! This the perfect moment to dust off those skeletons in the closet and to take a deeper look at the parts of yourself you normally hide. Too often, our fear keeps us from taking action. But as soon as you dare to delve deep into the shadows (even just for a little bit), the things you discover may not be scary at all!

WHAT HAVE YOU BEEN AFRAID
TO ADMIT TO YOURSELF?

TO OTHERS?

WHAT ARE YOU HIDING FROM THE WORLD?

WHAT DO YOUR FEARS AND BLOCKS STEM FROM? THINK BACK TO YOUR CHILDHOOD TO FERRET OUT THE ROOT CAUSE.

Your visions will become clear only
when you can look into your own
heart. Who looks outside, dreams;
who looks inside, awakes.

—Carl Jung

MINDFUL MOON

~~~~~~~~~~~~~~~~~~~

MAKE TIME TO FOR MINDFUL REFLECTION and soul searching in November: Go within, take a hike by yourself at dusk, meditate, take a night walk, sit in your garden at night . . . enjoy any activity where you can sit with yourself and nature. Being in the darkness of the night can be a supportive guide to going deeper within.

WHAT ACTIVITIES HELP YOU LIVE IN THE PRESENT AND GO DEEP WITHIN YOURSELF? LIST THEM BELOW.

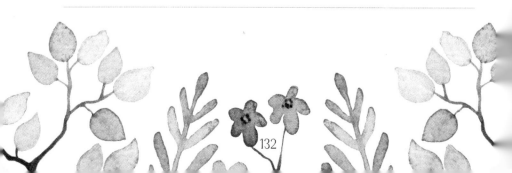

NEW MOON IN SCORPIO
INTENTIONS

TAKE A FEW MINDFUL MOMENTS TO REFLECT ON WHERE
you are now before you decide where to go next. Then set a few intentions
for this new moon.

WISH 1:

_____

_____

WISH 2:

_____

_____

WISH 3:

_____

_____

. . . stop a moment, cease your work, look around you.

—Leo Tolstoy

NOVEMBER MINDFULNESS & REFLECTIONS

WHAT THEMES & IDEAS ARE YOU
NOTICING OR EXPLORING THIS MONTH?

WHAT PATTERNS AND FEELINGS ARE YOU NOTICING
IN YOURSELF?

WHAT WORKED & DIDN'T WORK IN YOUR MAGICK
OVER THE LAST MONTH?

DECEMBER
THE LONG NIGHT MOON

In December, the darkness prevails over the light! This full moon is named after the longest night of the year, which occurs at the end of this month. But even when we're bathed in darkness, we know that the sun will gain strength and dominance. This is a beautiful time for reflection on both the year behind you and the year ahead.

WHAT DOES THE MONTH OF DECEMBER MEAN TO YOU?

WHAT WERE YOUR PERSONAL HIGHLIGHTS THIS YEAR?

Magic lies in challenging what seems impossible.

—Carol Moseley Braun

Sabbat: Yule

(DECEMBER 21 OR 22)

It's celebration time! Yule, also referred to as Midwinter, is the longest night and shortest day of the year. On these dark days, we shift our attention to what's ahead of us. It's time to anticipate the return of the light. Yule is a holiday centered around renewal, hope, and celebration for all.

HOW CAN YOU SHOW YOUR APPRECIATION TO THOSE IN YOUR LIFE? OR TO THE SPIRIT WORLD?

WHAT ARE YOU THE MOST GRATEFUL FOR THIS YULE?

_____

_____

_____

_____

_____

_____

_____

Mindful, Magickal December Activities

• Make charitable donations or volunteer your time.

• In these dark days, it's time to celebrate a primitive and powerful source of light: fire! Whether you light candles or a fireplace, igniting a flame is a beautiful way to celebrate the season.

Magickal Correspondence

ELEMENT:
Fire

COLORS:
Black, white, and red call to mind the darkness of the season.

STONES:
Think dark and rich, like ruby, obsidian, and serpentine.

GODS:
Athena, Persephone, Osiris, and Hades are
a natural fit for the darkest time of the year.

HERBS:
Get seasonal with mistletoe, holly, berries, and cinnamon.

JOT DOWN YOUR OWN IDEAS FOR
DECEMBER CORRESPONDENCES HERE:

NEW MOON
IN SAGITTARIUS

SAGITTARIUS IS SYMBOLIZED BY THE CENTAUR. THIS GIVES us a beautiful reminder to keep our feet firmly grounded while we shift our attention up to the stars! The new year is almost upon us! This is the perfect time to reflect on the past year and plan for the year ahead.

In the beginning of the month, your desires and intentions might seem a little crazy! You're aiming in the dark, perhaps unable to see where you're heading. It's important to trust your instincts and desires in this moment more than it is to have everything perfectly mapped out.

WHERE ARE YOUR DESIRES STEERING YOU RIGHT NOW? (DON'T GET CAUGHT UP ON WHAT YOU USED TO WANT.)

IF YOU COULD MAKE ANYTHING HAPPEN IN THE YEAR AHEAD, WHAT WOULD IT BE?

NEW MOON IN SAGITTARIUS
INTENTIONS

~~~~~~~~~~~~~

TAKE A FEW MINDFUL MOMENTS TO REFLECT ON WHERE you are now before you decide where to go next. Then set a few intentions for this new moon.

WISH 1:

_____

_____

_____

_____

WISH 2:

_____

_____

_____

_____

WISH 3:

_____

_____

_____

DECEMBER
MINDFULNESS
& REFLECTIONS

WHAT THEMES & IDEAS ARE YOU
NOTICING OR EXPLORING THIS MONTH?

_____

_____

_____

_____

WHAT PATTERNS AND FEELINGS ARE YOU NOTICING
IN YOURSELF?

_____

_____

_____

_____

WHAT WORKED & DIDN'T WORK IN YOUR MAGICK
OVER THE LAST MONTH?

_____

_____

_____

_____

My Grimoire

THE HONEY JAR

~~~~~~~~~~~~~~~~~~~~~~~~~~~~~~~~~~~

THIS CLASSIC SPELL CAN BE USED TO ATTRACT OUTCOMES, people, and physical things into your life.

You'll need:

a glass jar with a metal lid

honey
(vegans can use an
animal-friendly substitute)

paper & pen

candle

Start off by writing down the appropriate names on the paper. If the spell is just for you, just your name will suffice. If you're healing a relationship or wanting to warm things up with someone, then write both names down. Write the names directly on top of each other but flip the paper around so they each face a different direction.

Next, it's time to write your petition: your ideal outcome. Write it in a circle around and around on the page. The idea here is to not lift the pen during the writing process, so pick a short phrase that encompasses what you want to happen. (Use "love and blessings," for example.)

Once the paper has been filled up with your wishes, it's time to fold the paper into threes. (You can also anoint it with a special oil if you feel so inclined!)

Add the paper to the jar then add your honey (or sugar mix) on top. You can also get creative here and add in any extra roots or herbs (I suggest cinnamon!). Keep adding the honey until your petition is completely covered.

Then put the lid on the jar and place your candle on top. Think again of your intention as you light the candle, and try to keep it lit as long as you can!

You can also add this jar to your altar and feel free to light more candles on top of it in the future, if you feel so called.

AN EASY MONEY SPELL

You'll need:

a green candle

cinnamon

six coins

a green cloth or pouch

your choice of essential oil

Set up your altar, including any other elements that seem to fit. Pause and meditate for a few minutes to collect your energy before you begin.

Anoint your candle with the essential oil. Place the candle on your altar and arrange the six coins around the candle in a circle. As you place each coin, visualize yourself receiving money. Get into an attitude of gratitude!

Once you've placed each coin, light the candle while you repeat this incantation three times:

"Money does flow,
Money does grow.
My money does shine.
The money is now mine."

Then lay out your green cloth. Sprinkle some cinnamon on top, then wrap the coins in the cloth (or place them in the pouch). As you pick up the coins, use this chant three times:

"Bring me money three times three,
As I will it, so mote it be."

Fold up the cloth or pouch and place it in your purse or bag, where it can be with you at all times.

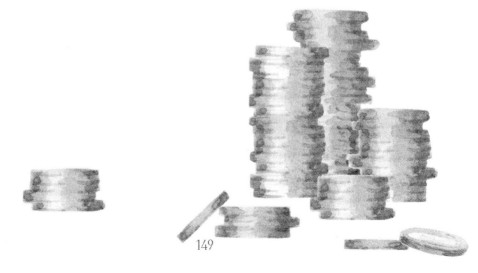

A SIMPLE PROTECTION SPELL

SALT IS THE CLASSIC CHOICE FOR PROTECTION, ESPECIALLY in the home! This simple spell protects your home and its inhabitants from negative energy entering the space.

You'll need:

salt

(Optional: the full moon.
But any time of the month will work!)

All this spell involves is moving around your space in a circle, sprinkling salt on the perimeter as you go. (You can do this either indoors or out! If you do it indoors, be very sparing with the salt or try to leave it alone for as long as possible before you vacuum or sweep up.) Visualize white light or protective energy surrounding your space as you go.

If you like, use an incantation to go along with this:

"Protect this home and all who reside here."

Finish things off by declaring,

"This house is now protected from negative energies and forces. So mote it be!"

She's always had
the power. . . .
She had to find it
out for herself.

—Glinda (the Good Witch),
The Wizard of Oz

Book of
Shadows

A Book of Shadows is simply a book that helps a witch keeps track of her intentions, favorite spells, and rituals. It's important to record your spells so you can evaluate their effectiveness and refer back when you need to use them again.

Spell Notes:

_____

_____

Intention:

_____

_____

Supplies:

_____

_____

Incantation:

_____

_____

How To:

_____

_____

Spell Notes:

_____

_____

Intention:

_____

_____

Supplies:

_____

_____

Incantation:

_____

_____

How To:

_____

_____

Spell Notes:

_____

_____

_____

Intention:

_____

_____

_____

Supplies:

_____

_____

_____

Incantation:

_____

_____

_____

How To:

_____

_____

_____

Spell Notes:

Intention:

Supplies:

Incantation:

How To:

Spell Notes:

_____

_____

_____

Intention:

_____

_____

_____

Supplies:

_____

_____

_____

Incantation:

_____

_____

_____

How To:

_____

_____

_____

Spell Notes:

_____

_____

_____

Intention:

_____

_____

_____

Supplies:

_____

_____

_____

Incantation:

_____

_____

_____

How To:

_____

_____

_____

Spell Notes:

Intention:

Supplies:

Incantation:

How To:

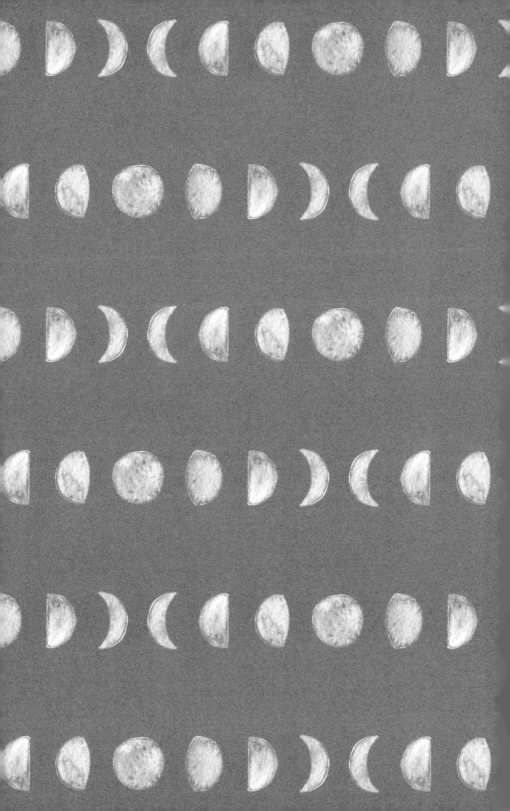